The Essential Guide to Family Business Succession

BLACK BOX SUCCESSION

THE SURPRISING TRUTH ABOUT FAMILY BUSINESS

The Essential Guide to Family Business Succession

BLACK BOX SUCCESSION

THE SURPRISING TRUTH ABOUT FAMILY BUSINESS

RAKESH SHARMA

INDIA'S #1 SUCCESSION GURU FOR FAMILY BUSINESS

Worldwide Published by

Pendown Press

PENDOWN PRESS

An ISO 9001 & ISO 14001 Certified Co.,

Regd. Office: 2525/193, 1st Floor, Onkar Nagar-A,

Tri Nagar, Delhi-110035

Ph.: 09350849407, 09312235086

E-mail: info@pendownpress.com

Branch Office: 1A/2A, 20, Hari Sadan, Ansari Road,

Daryaganj, New Delhi-110002

Ph.: 011-45794768

Website: PendownPress.com

First Edition: 2023

ISBN: 978-93-5554-519-0

Contents

About Author

Rakesh Sharma is on a quest to help family business owners build lasting legacies. He works with a select group of family businesses to help them get clear on their Succession. He is the creator of the '100 Years Legacy Model' program for family businesses, which provides practical tools to help family businesses be healthier.

Acknowledgement

I am incredibly grateful to my mentors Akshar Yadav & Siddharth Rajsekar for their support in bringing this book to life. Their input and feedback were invaluable, and I couldn't have done it without them.

I feel so fortunate to have had Shubhi, my daughter by my side throughout this writing process. Her insights and ideas have been invaluable, and I can't thank her enough for all that she has done.

Who Am I On This Journey

You're about to spend some time with this handbook. You might as well know who wrote it before you dig in.

Here are a few things about me. I...

- have a passion for helping family businesses build lasting legacies,

- have a passion for helping family businesses be healthier and more functional,

- don't think family businesses have to be full of drama,

- have over a dozen years of experience working with the owners and leaders of family businesses,

- have a guiding purpose in life to make a huge difference in the world now and for generations,

- run a business with the purpose of helping 1,00,000 family businesses get healthier,

- have a certification in coaching and training,

- am a Chartered Accountant, Author, Speaker & Mentor with experience of more than 26 years.

Here are a few more things about me. I...

- will share tools & process, on how I engaged my kid to join family business,

- don't have much patience for people who want to perpetuate dysfunction in their business,

- don't think helpful hand books need to be long.

MY INSPIRATION

For over a dozen years, I have had the honor of talking with owners and leaders of family businesses. Many times, I have seen decisions being made in the business by the single most influential family member i.e. without getting consent of other family members. Sadly, many of these decisions have been detrimental to the business and in the end, hurt the family too.

In most cases, these influential members do not realize that the thing they are fighting for, is precisely the reason the business and family are suffering.

These are decisions such as:

- How much money the next generation should make?

- Who should own the business?

- Who should run the business?

- Can family members get fired?

- Who should work in the business and in which job?

- & many more...

Often, the spouse is trying to help. They are fighting (sometimes yelling) for what they believe is the best thing for their family.

This handbook is made for business owners who want a resource that helps them influence the family business in a way that is positive for the family and business.

Chapter 2

Why Succession Planning is Important in Family Businesses!

Kavi Rathore, the eldest of the third generation from a middle-class, closely knit Joint Family of the Rathore's. His father, mother, two uncles, their wives and children all lived under one roof in Delhi. He had big dreams and wanted to make a name for himself in the world. So, after his graduation from Delhi he landed a job as a consultant in the USA and moved there.

The patriarch of Kavi's family, his grandfather, was still alive. He was a wise man, and he wished to see his family prosper. So, he sent some money to Kavi in the USA and asked him to starts an automobile business there.

Kavi worked hard for a few years managing two jobs, a consultant during the day and an auto mobile-maker by night, and he put his everything into building the business. Over time, the business took off, and he acquired one more manufacturing factory.

More of his family members immigrated to the USA to support the growing business, and Kavi also gave up the consulting job and began working in the business full-time.

The scale of the business was premium and the business was highly successful.

Besides investing money in the automobile sector in the USA, Kavi's grandfather also sent one of his sons to Bengaluru with some money to start a Chimney business. That business also took off through a great combination of luck and hard work. In a few years, they became India's big brands of chimney makers.

With time, one day, the grandfather passed away, and the brothers continued living with their families in Delhi. There was growing unease, though. In the old man's time, there was an honour-bound contract that the family wealth would be equally distributed among the three brothers.

Those were days when words were way more powerful than any paper contract.

However, when the businesses were incorporated, Kavi's name was not on the paperwork for some reason.

With time, things began changing, and the familial bonds were not as cordial as before.

Kavi started feeling uneasy. As the business kept growing, so did his unease. One day he broached the subject of asset allocation with his uncles. He did not ask for his share or a split in the business. All he asked for was some paperwork that gave clarity on what he owned.

To his utter shock, the elder uncle frostily and untruthfully proclaimed, ''These factories are mine. I am grateful for your services. I can calculate the salary for your work and pay that off with interest. But don't harbour any illusions of equity in the business. It was my share of the money that was invested, and the paperwork also says so."

That was it.

In one statement, Kavi was finished. He couldn't come to terms with the betrayal and took to drinking and started wasting away his life.

Then he decided to travel to India and approach his other uncle, the chimney maker and request him to share that business. It was a more cordial conversation with the uncle in India, but the result was the same. Kavi was courteously shown the door.

Distraught and defeated, he returned to USA and went into depression. Finally, with nothing to show for his hard work, he fell back on his consulting job to make a living.

So, why am I sharing this painful story, you might be wondering?

I share this story as a wake-up call to all family businesses and especially their current heads.

Make sure that as wealth grows in the family, timely Succession Planning is MUST for substantial Family Alignment.

Chapter 3

What Exactly is a Family Business?

Before we move any further, let's first understand a Family Business.

A Family Business is any business where more than one member of a family takes on management or active ownership responsibility. You have a family business if you work with someone in your family in a business you both own or which you may someday own.

The essence of a family business is that blood, work, and business ownership are common.

There are two major types of family businesses: **single-generational and cross-generational.** (Refer Diagram 1)

Single-generation family businesses begin when one entrepreneur invites other family members of their generation to share the management/ownership of the business or when two relatives of the same generation start a business. It may be two brothers, cousins, or a couple.

The line is crossed when one relative asks another not just to help out but to take on major responsibility with the expectation of a share of ownership in the future. **Traditionally,** many small businesses were started by brothers or male cousins. Today, women are increasingly being part of family businesses.

The **most frequent new pattern in single-generational businesses is the couple-owned business.** This is a family business where a couple not only works together but where the business is seen as a shared responsibility (if not always equally shared). Couples in business together have their own set of problems, mainly around separating work and personal life and avoiding destructive conflict and competition.

Cross-generational family businesses usually arise later in a business's life cycle, when the founding generation has grown the business to the point where it can accommodate the next generation.

Less frequently, such businesses are started by pairs, often a father and son. The complexity of cross-generational family businesses stems from two essential tasks:

- Modifying the parent-child relationship into one of peers at work.

- Preparing the younger generation to take over leadership.

Struggles between parent and child, or between different branches of the family, often create pain and drama and threaten the future of the business and sometimes the family too. **Since both businesses and families have their evolving life cycles, problems arise when the business and family life cycles are not in sync.**

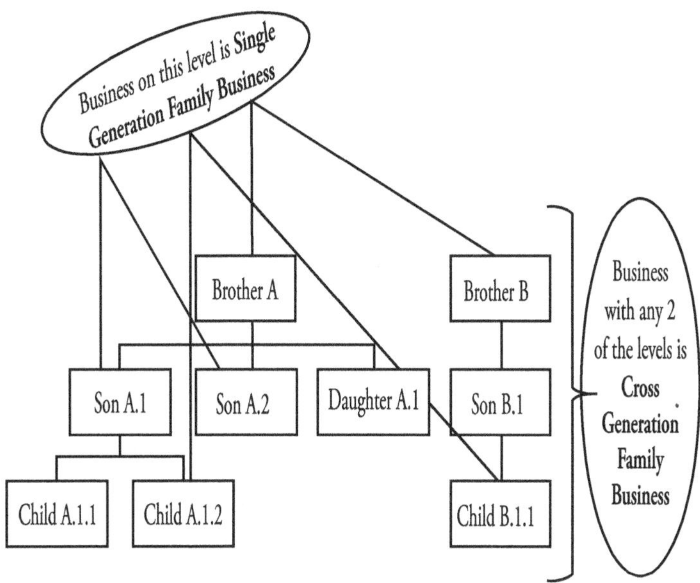

Diagram 1: Single and Cross-Generation Family Businesses

Family Work Relationships

In a rough survey of over 100 family businesses, from case accounts and my own experience, the family relationships reported in both single and cross-generation Family Businesses are found to be as depicted in Diagram 2 and Diagram 3.

Single Generation

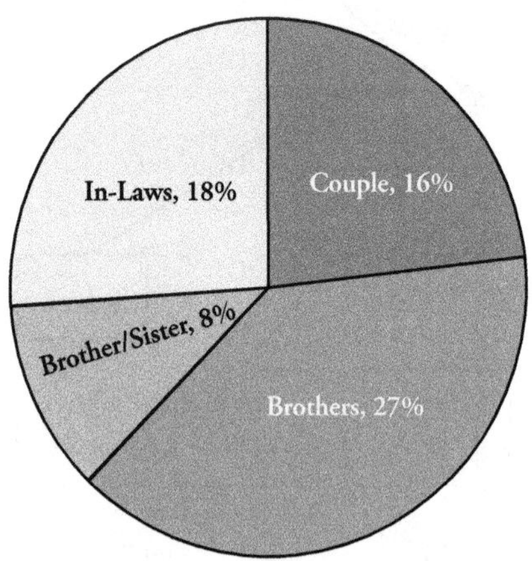

□ Couple, □ Brothers, □ Brother/Sister, □ In-Laws,

Diagram 2: Percentage-wise Family relationships in Single Generation Family Businesses

Cross Generation

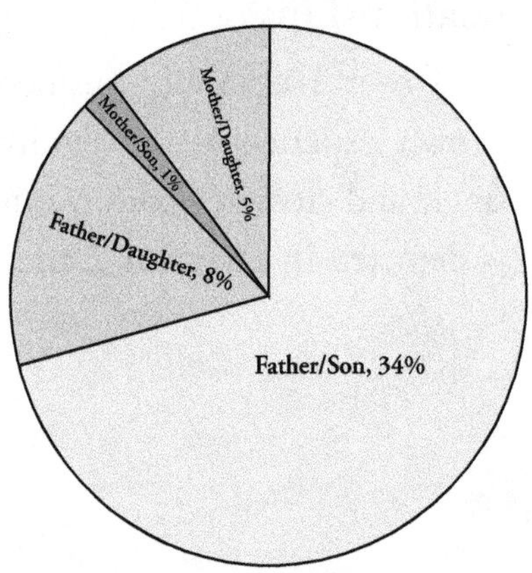

□ Father/Son □ Father/Daugter □ Mother/Son □ Mother/Daugter

Diagram 3: Percentage-wise Family relationships in Cross-Generation Family Businesses

Chapter 4

The Family That Plans Together Stays Together!

A leader's lasting value is measured by succession."
~John C. Maxwell

India is a country that thrives on family bonds. We nurture family above all else at all times, irrespective of any hurdles that may come our way. Family and its importance are woven deep into our social and moral fibre. Most Indians live, eat and breathe together as a family. The Joint Family System is our pride and joy. Our assets as a family are all held together. It is little wonder, then, that we do business as a family too.

The number of Family-owned Businesses in India is significant where; each generation proudly carries on the legacy of the family tradition of XYZ & SONS or XYZ BROTHERS!

However, such is the characteristic of life that it never stays the same. It comes with ups and downs, highs and lows, crests and troughs, and ebbs and flows. It takes great delight in throwing curve balls at us without warning and often takes us on a roller coaster ride.

Family Businesses are no exception to this rule of life!

Every head of the family sets up a business with the lofty intent of their heirs joining the business one day, expanding his legacy to even greater heights, and then proudly passing it on to the next generation just as they pass on values and traditions.

Sadly though, the scenario doesn't always play out according to plan!

Sometimes life decides to throw a spanner in the works!

Family Businesses, set up with a lot of love and hard work, can sometimes turn into battlegrounds littered with many casualties of in-fighting, litigation and soured relationships within the family that once lived, loved and laughed together.

Sometimes the situation turns so ugly, that the Bonds of Blood can lead to Bloodshed even.

Even if we take our focus off the worst-case scenario, the passing of the family business and other assets from one generation to another can cause a lot of confusion and chaos that can trigger the complete disintegration of the business as well as the family.

Picture the dilemma of a father of three sons who has spent his whole life building a successful company and a home worth crore of rupees. Now that it's time to pass on the torch to his three sons, how does he ensure an equal, fair, and amicable distribution of his assets so that the family and business do not disintegrate?

In another scenario, imagine the plight of the family that knows nothing about their son's intention not to join the family business. How should the son communicate his true feelings and preferences to his family without causing them distress? What should the family do to carry on the business smoothly while continuing to preserve their legacy?

I assure you things do not have to be so bad. There is a way out of these messy situations.

Yes, I can assure you of all the answers and solutions to these and other complex family-business issues that can crop up at any time, mostly unannounced!

And I can assure you of "SUPER BUSINESS GROWTH & FAMILY ALIGNMENT."

My name is Rakesh Sharma; **I am a qualified CA, Financial Consultant, Writer, Speaker and Family Business Mentor** with an extraordinary career spanning over two decades. I have been a friend, philosopher and financial guide to 2000+ entrepreneurs and counting. **During Covid times and onwards, i.e. in the last 3 years alone, I have empowered 100's of family-run enterprises all over India to Future-Proof their Business.** As a proven succession planning expert, I help enterprises to –

- Plan the family succession and business succession

- Cement cracks in shared family-business goals and family feuds

- Manage estate equalisation with a variety of tools such as Wills, Family Trust, Gift Deed, Relinquishment Deed, HUF Dissolution, Shareholding Agreement, Family Settlements etc.

- Distribute wealth and pass the family legacy to the next generation amicably

- Setting up Family Board and Family Office

- Preserve family legacy and goodwill

- Achieve financial prosperity

- Minimise the damages of unforeseen business contingencies

- Find future-proof solutions to their financial and familial business problems

- Protect themselves against anticipated and unanticipated risks

The one foolproof and future-proof solution to avoiding and smoothly navigating all the above-mentioned contingencies and chaotic scenarios is **"SUCCESSION PLANNING"**.

What is Future-Proof, you ask? It means a legacy for your family and business, for them to last, fighting all odds in the unforeseeable future!

Apart from my qualifications, vast experience, and massive success as a Financial Consultant, what fuels my passion for Succession Planning is my own story of **"Riches to Rags to Riches."**

I was an innocent boy of just 8 when my whole world came crashing down...

Born to an affluent, close-knit and happy joint family, I had everything one could ask for, thanks to my influential and successful grandfather, the family patron.

All was well in my world until the day my beloved grandfather passed away, and the joint family property turned into the bone of contention between my uncles and aunts.

Though my grandfather had a lot of land and possessions, they were unequally divided between his children and illegally kept by some of the siblings.

Soon after the patriarch's death, all the family members began to fight over the property and who would inherit what.

Sadly and shockingly, the family fight is still on, even after more than four decades!

My grandfather's failure to plan the family succession and future-proof his business unwittingly turned a loving family into a feuding family.

My father lost his share of the family property. Neither the Government nor lawyers could help him claim his rightful share because he chose not to fight with his siblings.

I had no legacy left to inherit from my grandfather except the love and wisdom he had freely bestowed on me during our short time together.

This, coupled with the values instilled in me by my parents, has stood me in good stead all my life.

Not bogged down by life's experiences, I saw how my parents worked hard to restart their life and build their legacy from scratch. Drawing inspiration from my parents, I, too, established myself from the ground up.

Once established firmly, I vowed to help family businesses and families avoid making the grave mistake that my grandfather had made.

Today, I am successfully helping numerous family businesses to put an end to their family feuds and become future-ready, as I do not want to see any family disputes in my clients' lives.

I am on a mission to educate and sensitize more and more Indian family business owners about the importance of **timely Succession Planning** so that what happened to my family does not happen to anyone ever again.

CASE STUDY 1

Painful Downturn of Poor Succession Planning

It is not just my story, but a story that is common in many family-business across the globe. Have you heard about the Feud in Gucci or the Viacom Saga?

☞ *Refer to the Case Study in the appendix at the end for more details.*

The importance and benefits of Succession Planning cannot be emphasised enough.

So, if you run a family-owned business and have joint assets, you cannot afford to miss this book.

In the next chapter, we will dive into a deeper understanding of what exactly Succession Planning is.

> *No Matter the Company Size, Revenue or Sector, Family Business Succession is never easy, and no two Successions are the Same.*

What Is Succession Planning?

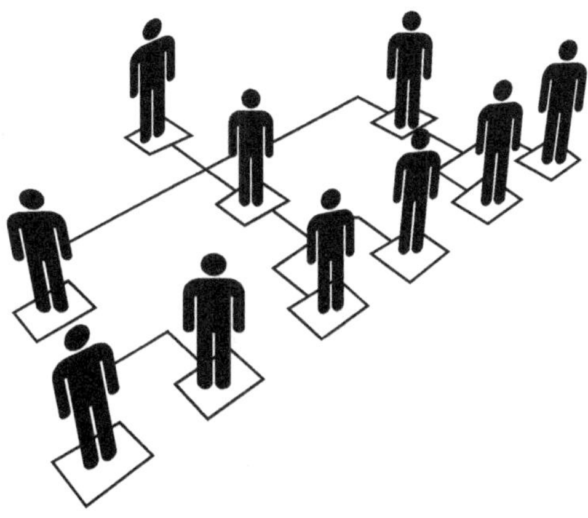

Now that we have established the critical importance of Succession Planning, the next logical step is to understand what Succession Planning is all about.

- What it encompasses?

- How does it work?

- What are the benefits?

You may have casually heard of the term 'Succession Planning', but most business owners do not know what it means and what its ramifications are, especially for family-owned businesses.

You could be the best businessman of your lifetime; you could have built a huge empire with your expansive vision, diligent effort and intelligent business acumen, but like the quote that we started the book with, your true measure of leadership in the business and the family is decided by the way you handle the Succession of your empire and your family.

If you fail to ensure a smooth Succession transition process, all your hard work will likely go down the drain.

Business Succession Planning encompasses:

- All those essential and systematic planning processes that every family-run business must follow to build and grow their business.

- As well as identify, define and plan the legal Succession of your business in a timely and transparent manner. It is meant to help prepare your business for all contingencies by preparing high-potential leaders to take over when needed.

The aim of Succession Planning is to leave nothing to chance when it comes to finding the most suitable person to succeed in the footsteps of the business head/business owner. Creating a Succession Plan is a proven way to help minimize turbulence while transitioning the business from one generation to another, and define the manner in which the assets you own should be shared/distributed amongst your heirs.

It is a planned and meticulous way that future-proofs your business and family's prosperity and integrity.

A Succession Plan is not merely limited to the smooth Succession transitioning of the business and other assets into the next generation!

An excellent succession plan can ensure the protection of your legacy for several generations and hundreds of years.

A Succession Plan is meant to help you (Refer Diagram 4)–

- Preserve your hard-earned wealth and legacy for your future generations for hundreds of years to come.

- Choose which factors to consider while shortlisting the most desirable individuals to carry your legacy forward.

- Train and nurture the next generation to become true leaders and beacons of your business philosophy during your lifetime.

Diagram 4: How a Succession Plan can help you

With the help of timely Succession Planning, family-run businesses can eliminate all kinds of obscurities surrounding –

- How to transfer ownership of the business after the retirement or death of the owner?

- How to ensure a smooth transfer and transition from the retiring business head to the next generation of leaders?

- How to divide the inheritance among the legal heirs and family members?

- Who holds the decision-making power?

- What is the role of the different family members in the business?

- Who is the most eligible business successor based on shared business visions, leadership skills, education, experience, and relationship, as well as how to train them well?

- How to minimise all chances of internal conflicts between family members?

- What happens when certain family members want to sell their stake in the business?

- How to ensure that the key employees stay with the firm even after the management changes hands?

Succession Planning is the only Future-proof method you can use to remove all kinds of surprises/shocks or loopholes that can destroy the legacy you have worked so hard to build.

Another characteristic of Succession Planning is that it is NOT a one-size-fits-all scheme. Succession Planning is entirely customisable; the plan takes into account all the things that are unique to your business and your family. It is built around YOUR Vision and YOUR Wishes while keeping all legalities and compliances in mind to give you the solution that is best for you.

All it takes is choosing the right Succession Planning Advisor/Consultant because generations' worth of hard work, wealth and legacy are at stake.

Think of it this way.

A farmer preps his fields, builds a scarecrow and invests in good-quality fertilisers to nourish his fields much before sowing the seeds. He does it to ensure that his fields are prepared to yield healthy produce year after year.

Similarly, your business, too, needs the protection and preservation of a well-drafted and Future-proof Succession Plan.

CASE STUDY 2

Tools of Succession Planning

*Mr. GM Rao, the founder of **GMR Group**, a Family Business, has successfully set up a Family Constitution and created a Family Council back in 2002, through which it chooses the next generation of family members who would run the company and clearly define details like their compensation, specific roles and ways to resolve conflicts.*

It is one of the tools for preserving one's legacy.

☞ ***Refer to the Case Study in the appendix at the end for more details.***

Since the future is uncertain, we must prepare for any and every eventuality in advance. And the best technique to do it is to take the proper steps in the present so that the future of your business is in safe hands.

The wise have always emphasised that there is no time like the present. The present is our real present, our most precious gift. We are always taught that the right time to begin anything is Right NOW! So is the case with Succession Planning.

Remember, it is never too early to start planning your business succession if you want to leave behind a legacy for your family members that they will be proud to call their own!

To secure your family's future, ACT Today!

Now that you have an understanding of the meaning of Succession Planning, in the following chapters, I will be sharing with you action steps to set the Succession Planning machinery into action and secure the future of your business.

First off, in the next chapter, we will look at the importance of Succession Planning in Family-Owned Businesses specifically.

Chapter 6

Succession Planning: A Must-Do for Family-Owned Businesses

While Succession Planning is essential for all organisations, it is all the more crucial for Family-Owned Businesses.

While other organisations have a plethora of options available to take on the mantle of leadership from a retiring leader. In a family-run business, this option is limited mainly to the biological heirs, and the emotional bonds that exist in a family, which makes choosing and announcing a successor rather complicated.

Visualise this scenario:

You have decided to retire; you announce your decision to your family, and your whole family is supporting you, cheering and congratulating you on the legacy you have built; you are also looking forward to spending more time with your family and living a laid-back life enjoying the fruits of your life-long labour of love.

But this could end up being just a dream that blows up in smoke within a few days of your retirement.

Can the day of your retirement be joyful when it arrives?

Maybe not!

Visualise another scenario

You are the stalwart of your family-owned business, and everything runs around you. You are the pillar keeping it all together; Life throws that curve ball we talked about in the introductory chapter, and suddenly you are hospitalized for an extended period and too weak to resume your duties.

WHAT NOW?

If you have not invested your time and effort into putting a Succession Plan into place, you could have the following questions robbing your happiness and peace of mind in both these scenarios (Refer Diagram 5):

- Should you sell off the business or let it continue?

- Who is going to carry your legacy forward and manage the business?

- Do your children even want to follow in your footsteps?

- Which one of your heirs is the most suited to step into your shoes?

- How will the ownership change hands?

- Have you saved up enough for your life post-retirement?

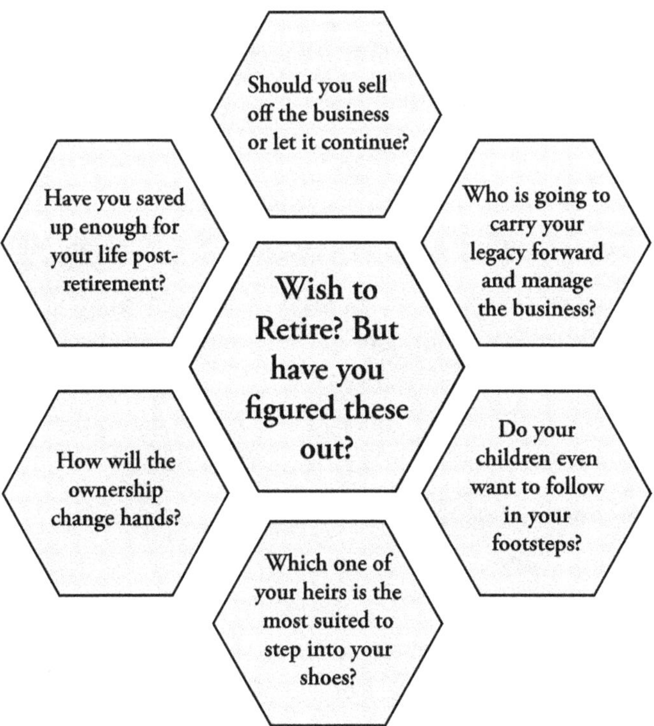

Diagram 5: Have you figured these out before planning your retirement from Business?

Research shows that a shocking 70% of Indian family-run businesses do not have a designated successor to lead the business forward after the retirement or sudden death of the business owner.

Once the founder passes away, the family inevitably gets pulled into **ugly disputes and tussles** of who will take over as the head of the business.

Often, family feuds continue for years and years, tarnishing your company's goodwill and destroying the integrity of your business.

It is for reasons such as these that timely business succession planning is so crucial for family-owned businesses.

A Succession Plan is like a GPS or an actionable blueprint that communicates and defines the vision of the business throughout several generations. It lays the groundwork for clearly demarcating the rights and responsibilities of the various family members based on their skill sets and vision.

Minimise Risks and Unpleasant Surprises with a Sound Succession Plan.

A family business is different from other businesses since family-run businesses are entrenched in deep familial ties and sentiments, which change the whole dynamics of business ownership.

That is why it's of paramount importance to commit to early and prompt formal succession planning, as it can help you avoid unnecessary in-family fights, hurt feelings and disappointments.

Succession planning is the best technique to ensure that your business continues to grow, prosper and pass on to worthy successors generation after generation, even long after you are no more.

Early Succession Planning is the Way Ahead

DID YOU KNOW? Research shows that India ranks No. 3 on the list of countries with the highest number of family-owned businesses globally.

Yet almost every family business today is struggling with some or the other form of dispute. What makes it worse is that most of these businesses fail to understand the urgency of planning their business succession, leaving everything to fate.

Regrettably, the term Succession Planning almost always comes up only when a business head passes away or retires, leading to far greater complications than solutions.

This is like firefighting once your house catches fire. While having a timely Succession Plan in place is akin to fireproofing your home, leaving a minimal chance that it could catch fire.

There are two primary reasons behind this mindset.

One, the owners don't wish to think that far ahead into the future, especially about their passing away or retirement. However, this is the biggest mistake they make! If anything is a constant in this ever-changing world, it is ageing and death. So why not prepare for the inevitable and plan ahead to ensure a smooth and stress-free transition for everyone?

The second reason is that most Family Business Owners just assume that their children will naturally follow in their footsteps and join the family business. So, they never foresee the need for a discussion to prepare and plan for either their children joining or not joining the business.

This, again, is a fatal mistake!

In life, nothing is a given. Your children are individuals with their own interests, aptitude, skillset and vision. They are free to make their own choices. A timely discussion about their career plans and an appropriate action plan accordingly can save both your business and your relationship with them.

CASE STUDY 3

A Lesson from the Predecessors

*We all recall the disagreements that ensued within the **Ambani Family** when Shri Dhirubhai Ambani passed away without a WILL, sparking years-long battles between the two sons.*

However, what is commendable is that Mukesh Ambani, having first-hand experience of the struggles and family disagreements, is on a path to set up his Succession Planning.

☞ *Refer to the Case Study in the appendix at the end for more details.*

Planning A Family Business Successor, Fuelling A Legacy

No matter how many strategies you may have developed to grow your business, the family business will collapse if you have not planned as to–

- How will the next generation share the family legacy?

- Who is qualified to lead the business once the family head passes away?

- How will the conflict amongst various branches of families, including issues on selling stakes by one branch of the family to a third party or within the family, be resolved?

- How will the successors take over the family business?

- How to train the successors so they can succeed in their new roles?

- How will those who run the business be compensated vis-a-vis those who are beneficiaries but not running the business?

You could very well lose your whole life's hard work and watch your business fail in front of your eyes, all because you did not protect your business against unforeseen contingencies.

If you haven't already, it is time to start your Business Succession Planning so you can ensure your family is well looked after and your business is in safe hands.

In the next chapter, before we dive into how to start Succession Planning, we will talk about the common mistakes people make when it comes to Business Succession Planning, so keep reading!

Succession Planning: Avoid These Common Pit Falls

At this juncture in the book, you are all aware that Business Succession Planning is an unavoidable and integral element of growing, building and running a successful family business.

If your business is family-owned and you hope to pass it on to your future generations smoothly, the first thing you need is a business succession plan; It's as simple as that!

Sounds simple! Yet, unless you have sound guidance in place, this simple task can turn into a catastrophe as big as not having a Succession Plan at all.

So, what goes wrong?

The first major mistake is **procrastination.** It is essential to **take timely action** and not wait until the last moment to set the wheels of a Succession Plan in motion.

Unfortunately, most business owners fail to understand its urgency and put it off for later, setting themselves up for failure and dangerous consequences.

Not having a Succession Plan in place for your hard-earned business is like building a beautiful sandcastle by the beach, too close to the sea and then hoping that the waves don't wash away your hard work.

Sometimes the damage is so extensive that business owners end up losing their whole life's work, and their children have nothing left to inherit.

Business owners offer many excuses for not having a Solid Succession Plan. Below I am enlisting the major ones.

Reasons Why Many Family Businesses Do Not Have A Succession Plan Yet.

Succession Planning is a term that raises numerous questions and doubts in the minds of many business owners. For others, it is a passing term that they don't pay much attention to. Some others even consider it a passing fad or trend, little realising how crucial it is to their overall well being.

Let's take a look at some reasons why succession planning is not a priority for some business owners (Refer Diagram 6)–

1. **Too Busy and Preoccupied:** As business leaders, you are often neck-deep in your day-to-day responsibilities.

In between making management decisions, expanding your business, networking and overseeing the staff, it is indeed challenging to find the time or the inclination to indulge in Succession Planning.

However, tell me, no matter how busy you are or how much in a hurry you may be, would you ever leave your home unlocked while going out? I am sure the answer is an emphatic NO!

Well, if your answer is No here, then how can you leave the business that you have worked so hard for unlocked and open to danger? No matter how busy you are, you must ensure you take the time out to protect your business from future risks through Succession Planning.

2. **Not Understanding the Urgency:** Many business owners feel they still have many years left until retirement, and there is no need to rush their business succession planning. This thought process is great, and of course, you will continue to take the business to greater heights long into the future.

    But despite being hale & healthy today, do you not buy health and life insurance to protect yourself and your loved ones?

    Do you not save up for your children's future or your old age while still young?

    Here too, if you are delaying Succession Planning, you fail to consider unforeseen circumstances such as illness, accident or untimely death, which can completely reverse the business dynamics and lead to serious consequences in the absence of a formal Succession Plan.

An excellent and timely Succession Plan is the best and most Premium Insurance Plan you can have to protect your business from any such contingencies in the future.

3. **Lack of Correct Knowledge and Help:** So many business owners are unaware of the importance of succession planning and how crucial it is for the safety, security and longevity of their family business. In the absence of the right knowledge and who to contact for help, businesses end up avoiding this significant aspect of running a family business.

    However, now that you have become aware of the importance of Succession Planning through this book, it becomes your moral duty to seek information and guidance and then work toward initiating your Succession Planning.

4. **Difficulty in Getting Started and Completing the Planning Process:** Succession Planning is a detailed and meticulous process. There are no shortcuts to Succession Planning if you want to do it right.

    Often, business heads lose their patience or become overwhelmed by the many facets of building a Succession Plan and give up midway. This is like

Harakiri or Suicide because the dangers of not having a Succession Plan are too many, and its benefits are simply too huge to ignore.

Since you have worked hard to build your business without shortcuts, do you not owe it to yourself and your loved ones to put in the same patience and perseverance to protect that business?

5. **Lack of Clarity:** Another big reason business owners shy away from Succession Planning is lack of clarity. Since it is a process that will eventually help you build a solid and safe business legacy for hundreds of years to come, it involves seeking answers to many complex questions and critical decision-making skills on your part. It also requires clear thinking and input from other family members.

    Sometimes, the family members may be at odds with one another, making it difficult to reach common ground, thus delaying the planning process.

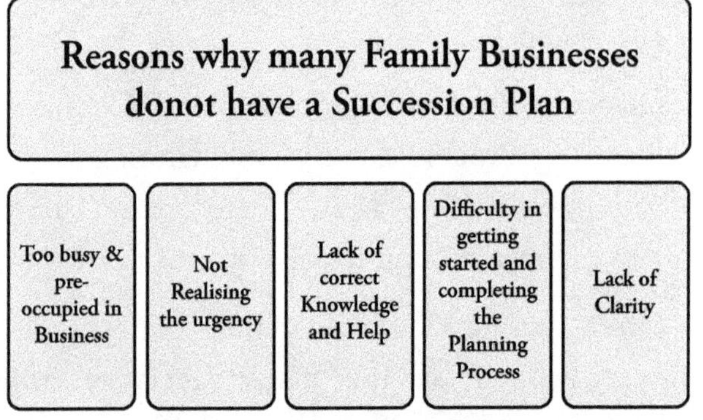

Diagram 6: Reasons Why Family Business do not have Succession Plan

However, your business is your legacy. It is worth protecting!

Don't let the above reasons rob you of your life's work!

Remember, **it is never too late to start** finalising your Business Succession Plan and **NOW** is a perfect time!

In the next chapter, we will understand the factors and action steps necessary to ace Succession Planning.

Chapter 8

Acing Succession Planning

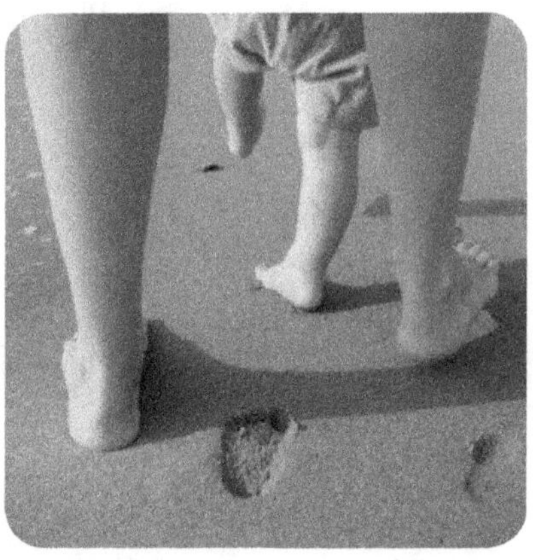

Big congratulations on your decision to start planning your business succession. It is the best decision you could have taken for the safety of your business and the peace and prosperity of your family for generations to come.

Succession Planning offers numerous benefits to businesses, especially those that are family-owned.

Finding the Best Person for the Job: With the help of a formal Succession Plan, you can narrow down your choice to the most qualified individuals to take over the reins when the important positions in your organisation become vacant due to retirement, illness or death.

Ready to Roll: And that's not all; timely Succession Planning will help you ensure that you have enough time to prepare and train your successors to step into their leadership roles. This ensures that the transition of leadership takes place with minimum disruption and maximum efficiency.

Let's work at understanding the main steps you need to follow to get your Succession Planning underway (Refer Diagram 7) –

1. **Identify Your Concerns:** Bringing clarity to kick-start the process of Succession Planning is of paramount importance. To get that clarity, the first thing you should do is to sit down and make a list of concerns and issues that you hope to address and solve through a Succession Plan –

    These could range to the following but are not limited to the same:

    a. How to protect the family members from internal tussles and litigations?

    b. How to ensure that loved ones are financially looked after, even when you're gone?

    c. How to retain key employees in your employment once you retire?

    d. How to identify the best individual who will become your successor?

    e. How to make sure the next generations will take your business to newer heights?

When you start the planning process with clarity, you are sure to develop a succession plan that is ideal for your organisation and its unique dynamic needs.

2. **Get the Most Suitable People Onboard:** No matter how clear and detailed your plan is, it can all come to nought without the right people on board.

    Since Succession Planning is crucial for your business's success and longevity, you must work with a strong team of individuals throughout the planning process. Look for people within the company who have foresight, knowledge, and the company's best interests at heart. You may also want to keep your family members in the loop to avoid last-minute complications or hurt feelings.

    And most importantly, consider bringing in a Succession Planning Expert to streamline and devise a winning succession plan for your family business.

    Succession Planning is not to be taken lightly. It is your entire legacy at stake for generations to come. Navigating the unique needs and challenges of your business and your family smoothly is best left to the experts. A Succession Plan is definitely not a DIY Project.

    The expert will personally coach and guide you through the complexities and hidden nuances of Succession Planning and help you pass on your business to capable successors amicably.

3. **Maintain Flexibility and Relevance:** Succession Planning is happening right now, but this plan is not just limited to a few years down the line. It is a plan spanning generations down the future. It cannot be rigid and watertight.

    Given the fast-altering market scenario, it is essential to make provisions in your succession plan for newer trends as and when they occur. Doing so will help you to draft a succession plan that is dynamic and flexible in nature and responds well to changing demands.

    While planning the Succession, use your company's core philosophies and overall vision as guiding forces to stay on track and ensure a winning plan that will lead your business towards unprecedented growth and a successful future.

4. **Pin-Point Possible Successors:** Carefully observe and understand your potential successors' interests, aptitude, and vision before narrowing down your list of possible successors to a few so that you can select the most suitable successor to lead your family business once you step down.

    Remember that while you may want all your children to get a share of the business, you can give just one child the power to run the business. Hence, it is good practice to talk to your family members so that you can find out their plans for the future and whether or not they wish to be involved in the family business.

CASE STUDY 4

Unique Innovation in Succession Plan

*In the case of the **Ranga Rao Family**, the family has been branching into new businesses rather than dividing the existing pie with the next generation.*

Isn't that an unique plan to maintain harmony in business and family?

☞ *Refer to the Case Study in the appendix at the end for more details.*

An excellent place to begin is to identify the qualities and skills you would like your successor to have. Next, make a list of the individuals in your family who possess the desired competencies and experience to carry your legacy forward.

5. **Groom your Successor/s:** Congratulations on selecting the ones who will be taking your business into the future. It's now time to train them to become worthy successors so that you can hand over the business to them with minimum disruption.

    Familiarise them with your Human Resources and your Infrastructure. Introduce them to your oldest employees, show them around the office and factory, share your vision and plans with them, acquaint them with your soft infrastructure, and get them up to date with your industry.

Step-wise guide to Succession Planning

Identify your Concerns	Get the most suitable People Onboard	Maintain Flexibility and Relevance	PinPoint Possible Successors	Groom your Successor/s

Diagram 7: Step-wise guide to your Business Succession Plan

Succession planning can take time and effort, but every minute you spend on it is well deserved and important for your business.

In the next chapter, we will understand the critical role open communication plays in the success of a Succession Plan.

Chapter 9

Succession Planning: Open Communication is the Key

Effective communication is the key to success in business as well as relationships. Since Succession Planning is a complex mix of business and relationships, communication plays a very vital role in its success.

Your business succession is an integral part of building and running a successful business that you can proudly hand over to future generations. And when you keep the lines of communication open, you automatically ensure that your entire family is not only on board with the planning process, but there are also minimal chances of disruption or hurt feelings later on.

Open communication is the critical difference between Confusion and Clarity.

Many of you might have observed that a lot of family businesses end up spending too much time on in-family fights and disputes, which take away the focus from the welfare of the business and put the family name in jeopardy.

The reason behind this is the lack of open communication. The in-fighting and chaos are because they did not communicate with one another clearly and transparently.

Let it not happen to your family business!

Communicating Your Way Through Business Succession Planning

In the following section, I will guide you through the right way of communicating with your family to ensure that your Succession Planning is a complete success.

INITIAL DISCUSSIONS–ONE-ON-ONE is the way to go.

So, you have set the wheels of Succession Planning in motion, and you now have a clear idea of how things will proceed. It's time to start talking it over with your family members.

Given that they may be unaware of your decision to begin the crucial process of family-business Succession, it could act as a Nuclear Weapon wreaking havoc on the entire family if not communicated properly.

It would be a good idea to break the news to them gently, preferably on a one-on-one basis. It will give each person the freedom to express their opinions openly to you without worrying about others' opinions.

During such interactions, do watch out for signs of how each person reacts to the news and note their inputs, as this will come in handy later and can be the difference between a successful and unsuccessful plan.

For example, in your conversations, you may find out that the person you were counting on to manage your business after your retirement has plans of their own and is not even interested in working for the family business!

The Next Stage –Getting Them All Together

Once you have completed the initial discussions with your family members separately, it's now time to come together as a family and talk about business finances as well as the direction you want to give your business.

Unfortunately, so many family businesses are losing the art of communication. However, suppose you want your Business Succession Planning to give you the best results. In that case, it is imperative to revive family meetings and communicate openly with each other, especially about the company's overall mission and how each member should contribute to this mission.

A good idea would be to start with a **family meeting**, say every three months, during which all the attendees can ask questions or express their concerns. It is also a good opportunity to analyse the progress of the Succession Plan and define or modify the future course of action based on the review.

Another good thing about family meetings is that they provide a common platform for each individual to discuss the issues that are bothering them. A timely resolution makes all the difference, whereas unspoken resentment can lead to disharmony and the disintegration of the entire plan.

Take the example of four brothers who have been running their family business for over 20 years. Since the brothers were always fighting over some issue or another, the company's brand value had hit ZERO. As a result, the next generation was unwilling to join such a disrupted family business.

It was here that clear communication saved the business. After the alignment of the four brothers with their shared family goals and values and the creation of a written Governance Module for the company and family, peace was finally restored. With this change in scenario, even their kids were now willing and excited to join the family business to carry the legacy forward.

CASE STUDY 5

Two Families running One Family Business!

*The **Emami Group** has mastered this art of communication, by integrating not just one but two Families, in one Family Business. Yes! The promotors were friends hailing from two different Marwari families in Kolkata.*

With the second generation already handling the business, the bond between the two families is simply commendable. The key being effective communication!

☞ *Refer to the Case Study in the appendix at the end for more details.*

Involve The Expert

Succession Planning is an essential process, unique to each family, that the family often tends to delay. It is, however, highly recommended not to. The benefits are too many to miss out on and the losses too high to ignore.

You can definitely try to DIY (Do It Yourself), but it is not at all advisable! It is important to have an expert guide you through the process.

Drafting A Winning Succession Plan – Bring In The Expert

Since emotions and sentiments are a part of the family business dynamics, it is not only wise but essential to involve a neutral person who can take the communication forward in the right direction objectively and fairly, considering each person's point of view.

Consider hiring a Succession Planning expert who is adept at guiding businesses through the complications of succession planning in a hassle-free and smooth way.

Remember, businesses that benefit the most from Succession Planning are those that focus on transparent and open communication.

To Summarise the process...

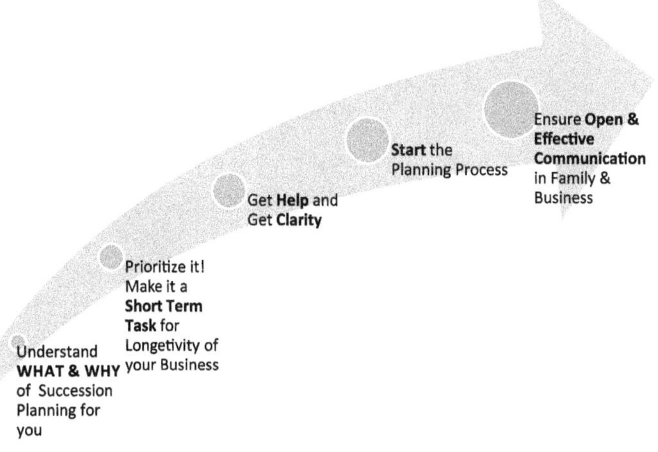

Diagram 8: Ready reference for Succession Planning process

Succession Planning:
Your Time Starts Now!

There is no right or wrong time to plan your business succession. However, the sooner you start succession planning, the more successful you will be in safeguarding the future of your business and legacy.

In the previous chapters, we have talked about the core elements that go into Business Succession Planning. Here is a quick recap –

- **Business Succession Planning** encompasses all those essential and systematic planning processes that every family-run business must follow to build and grow their business and identify, define and plan the legal Succession of their business in a timely and transparent manner.

- **Succession planning** leaves nothing to chance in searching for the most suitable person to walk in your footsteps. It ensures that your family is well looked after and your business is in safe hands.

- **Businesses delay the succession planning** process because they are too busy with their day-to-day responsibilities, don't have clarity or fail to understand the urgency of timely succession planning.

- **The right way to do succession planning** is to start early. Get the right people on board, list down the key concerns, identify your successors and start grooming them for the future.

- **Communicate clearly and openly** with your family members for a successful succession planning experience.

And as we have already discussed, Succession Planning is not a DIY project; it is a complex, sensitive, and essential process. However, there is no need to be hesitant or unsure about the process.

With an expert hand holding you through the process, there is no reason you cannot Ace it.

As shared earlier, I have already helped numerous business owners successfully implement Succession Plans and bid goodbye to unnecessary stress and uncertainty forever.

My mission is to help as many business owners as possible to protect their legacy through careful Succession Planning.

Now that you understand the critical necessity of Succession Planning, it is time to take the first step.

*Are you ready to start building
your formal succession plan?*

Next Step

My Workshop on Succession Planning as India's First Succession Guru for Family Businesses is sold out in advance.

However, as a reader of this book, I believe that you are serious about protecting your legacy and are making an effort to learn more & more about it. I urge you to visit us at **http://rakesh-sharma.com** to watch out for the date of the forthcoming session & book your spot! If you are ready for Personalised Mentorship with me use the below details to get the ball rolling!

Now that you have already climbed the first step on this beautiful journey; ensure that you keep going till you have immortalized your Family Business!

✶✶✶

Start Super Business Growth and Family Alignment NOW!

Join The Personliased Family Business Mentorship

 meet@rakesh-sharma.com

FB.com/Rakesh.SuccessionGuru

Case Study Appendix

INDEX

CASE STUDY 1

Painful Downturn of Poor Succession Planning **–Gucci & Viacom**

CASE STUDY 2

The Potential of Timely Succession Planning **–GMR Group**

CASE STUDY 3

A Lesson from the Predecessors **–Ambani Family**

CASE STUDY 4

Unique Innovation in Succession Plan **–NR Group**

CASE STUDY 5

Two Families running One Family Business! **–Emami Group**

Painful Downturn of Poor Succession Planning

–GUCCI & VIACOM

CASE 1 A: THE GUCCI FEUD

Gucci is a world-renowned name in the realm of fashion & lifestyle, but they faced many challenges that threatened their business due to a lack of Succession Planning.

Guccio Gucci, the founder, started the company in Florence in the early 20th century. Initially launched the business with his line of premium-quality luggage and hand bags. With Guccio's death in 1953, the business passed on to Aldo, the oldest of his three sons. Aldo had big plans and quickly expanded the company to major markets outside Italy. This established Gucci as an international name in fashion.

The Guccis are an example of how, without a clear direction for the future of the company, problems can arise when the next generations harbour conflicting ambitions.

Later on, Aldo's son Paolo ambitiously wanted to launch a new fashion line. However, his father and uncle were not on board with the idea. Still, he went ahead and launched it behind their backs. As a result, he was fired and exiled from the family business.

Things turned really ugly when Paolo sought revenge by exposing Aldo's tax issues. This eventually led Aldo to serve a year in federal prison for tax evasion.

In time, Paolo and his cousin Maurizio teamed up to take over the business. But without a clear plan, the cousins nearly ran the established business aground.

Paolo launched another disastrous fashion line, and when Maurizio had sole control of the company, Gucci had a negative net worth of $17.3 million.

With more than $40 million in personal debt, Maurizio was finally forced out of the company by Investcorp.

CASE 1 B: THE VIACOM SAGA

Without a clear Succession Plan, the events triggered by the Succession battle of Sumner Redstone for the controlling interest in Viacom turned as complicated as the incredible Game of Thrones saga.

To give you some background, Redstone owns 80 per cent of National Amusements Inc. (NAI), which in turn owns both CBS Corp. and Viacom. Viacom is a media conglomerate that controls Paramount Pictures and major U.S. cable stations such as MTV, BET and Comedy Central, to name a few.

Sumner's daughter Shari owned the remaining 20% of NAI, and her eventual Succession seemed natural.

However, things took a turn for the ugly in 2007 when Sumner and Shari began washing their dirty linen in public.

As a result, instead of naming Shari as his successor, Redstone chose to write an open letter to Forbes:

"While my daughter talks of good governance, she apparently ignores the cardinal rule of good governance that the boards of the two public companies, Viacom and CBS, should select my successor."

In a not-too-surprising move, in February 2016, Sumner Redstone's long-time right-hand Phillipe Dauman was named his successor as Chairman of Viacom and CBS. Shari, of course, was the only board member to vote against his appointment.

However, in a total movie-level thrilling turnaround three months later, Sumner and Shari teamed up to try to remove Dauman and his attorney George Abrams as board members of NAI.

This prompted a counter-suit by Dauman, who claimed that the senior Redstone's scheming daughter was manipulating him. Three months after that, Dauman resigned from his position.

Depending on the source, Shari Redstone has been in and out of power behind the scenes. There have been on-and-off plans to reunite CBS and Viacom, but the battle for control of the company continues to this day, and the picture keeps degenerating to new levels of low and ugly each month.

Source: Tharawat Magazine

The Potential of Timely Succession Planning

–GMR GROUP

Grandhi Mallikarjuna Rao came from a small town but had big dreams. He envisioned living in the port city of Visakhapatnam in a small house and a Fiat car. What seemed like big dreams at the time appeared very humble compared to what the first-generation entrepreneur has achieved to date.

At 65, his business was spread across airports, roads, power plants, and special investment regions, and his group owns infrastructure worth a whopping ₹67,000 crore. And there are more businesses in the pipeline. His foreign businesses include coal mines in Indonesia and the second largest airport in the Philippines- the Mactan-Cebu International Airport.

Though he has dabbled in nearly 28 businesses, including a brewery, ferro alloys, sugar mills, cotton bud manufacturing and IT, as things stand now, he has exited all non-infrastructure businesses except a jute mill in Andhra Pradesh.

He was also the largest shareholder with over 40 percent stake in the erstwhile Vysya Bank and later sold his stake to a Dutch banking corporation, the ING Group. The bank was renamed ING Vysya and was finally acquired by Kotak Mahindra Bank in 2014.

The Legacy Must Grow

As a first-generation entrepreneur, Rao obviously wanted to preserve what he has built and wanted to ensure that the coming generations focus on building on the legacy instead of quarrelling over the spoils.

Time and again, Rao had emphasised the need for Indian family businesses to always keep a distinction between Business and Family. Toward this aim, he set up a family council and created a family constitution as early as 2002.

The purpose of the council is to choose the next generation of family members to run the company and define their role, compensation, and conflict resolution processes.

Chairman, Rao had the final authority on all the family's business. The airports division helmed by his son-in-law Srinivas Bommidala as chairman, while his older son GBS Raju chairs the energy business, and his younger son Grandhi Kiran Kumar is the corporate chairman.

Rao has a plan for the evolving role of the family in the business. Right now, he sees the family at a stage where they are involved in every aspect of the business- strategy, public advocacy, relationships [with industry stakeholders], reviews and operations.

At a later stage, he only sees the family being involved in strategy, timely reviews and relationship building.

At the final stage of the evolution, he only sees the **family as an investor** providing strategy and direction as board members.

This is in keeping with the trends of family businesses in Europe and the US. They have always kept their businesses and personal interests separate.

Understanding the importance of timely succession practices and initiatives, the trend today, even with smaller family businesses, is to put in place a family structure **separating the family's personal assets from the business assets.**

And in another wise move, most family-owned businesses are **differentiating between ownership and management as two distinct functions.**

Another beneficial trend is first-generation promoters not forcing their children to join the business straight away though they continue to be owners. They encourage them to join only if they are interested. If and when they join the business, **their growth within the company is based on competence and is not a given by virtue of being owners.**

A Progressive Constitution

The GMR family constitution is an inclusive one; there is no election to the council. All family members of the first and second generations and their lineal descendants from the third generation onwards become members once they are 21 years old. All their women family members have equal rights in every matter. The constitution also gives a voice to everybody in the next generation.

The family council, a great succession planning tool, has proved to be a very constructive forum, giving members a chance to voice their concerns and resolve problems by communicating on a regular basis.

As per sources, there is a well-laid-out procedure in the family constitution, adopted unanimously by all family members, for the selection of a successor by the second generation at an appropriate time.

G.M. Rao is a pioneer in the business fraternity for setting up the family constitution. As per him, before setting up any family constitution, you need to create an alignment [of thought] among all family members, and he says it took him two years to do just that.

Almost everyone is taking a leaf out of their book as they probably have the most exhaustive constitution that deals with every eventuality that one could imagine. And they have put processes in place which they hope are timeless.

Source: Forbes India

A Lesson from the Predecessors

–AMBANI FAMILY

What transpired in the past!

I don't think any of us can easily forget the bitter family feud between the Ambani brothers Mukesh & Anil when their father Dhirubhai Ambani passed away without any clear directions.

With humble beginnings as a trading house in 1973, Reliance had grown into a full-blown empire by 2002, when Dhirubhai died without leaving a will.

This unfortunate eventignited an ugly battle for control of the empire between the brothers, who were both part of the business. After Dhirubhai's passing away, initially, Mukesh and Anil seemed to work together in harmony as chairman and vice chairman of Reliance, respectively.

However, cracks soon began showing up. They both believed that the other was not taking them into confidence while making critical decisions.

Things became so bad that, at one point, Anil even refused to put his signature on Reliance's financial statements. He cited inadequate disclosures as the reason behind this act. To make matters worse, the directors of a subsidiary that Anil ran tendered their resignations as a mark of solidarity, demonstrating their loyalty to Anil.

The real reasons behind the discontent were more psychological than professional. As the elder one, it was Mukesh's belief that he was the leader/boss by default. On the other hand, Anil did not subscribe to this, and he believed that they were both equal partners with equal rights and equal say.

This struggle for power literally degenerated into a civil war, and within three years of their father's death, their mother, Kokilaben, had to intervene and play referee.

In 2005 under Kokilaben's guidance, they reached a truce and agreed to divide their assets amicably. Anil was given the telecommunications, asset-management, entertainment and power-generation businesses, and Mukesh was given the petrochemicals, oil and gas, refining and textiles.

The Ambani Saga is the perfect unfortunate example of poor succession management.

Since Mukesh Ambani has been through such a bitter succession battle and learnt his lesson, he doesn't want a repeat of it for the next generation.

Creating a future-proof succession plan!

To prepare for the Succession of his next generation, Mukesh Ambani began studying other billionaire families, such as the Waltons and the Kochs and how they handled the process of passing on their legacy to the next generation, passed on what they'd built to the next generation.

After what he went through, Mukesh Ambani, with his 3 children & a $208 billion empire, cannot afford to be careless with his Succession planning. It would be one of the biggest wealth transfers in recent times.

According to sources in the know, Mukesh's plan has similarities with the Walton family of the Walmart group.

If sources are to be believed, Ambani might be putting his family's holdings into a trust-like structure.

Mukesh, with his wife Nita and three children, will be stakeholders in this new entity overseeing and being on its board, of course. This could also include a few of Ambani's long-term confidantes as advisers. Wisely enough, the management will mostly be entrusted to external professionals handling the day-to-day operations.

It appears that Mukesh has designed Reliance into three interlocking, but floatable businesses: digital, retail, and petrochemicals/energy and he and his wife are grooming their children to each take portions.

Source: Financial Times

Unique Innovation in Succession Plan

–NR GROUP, CYCLE AGARBATTI

Cycle Pure Agarbathies, the flagship brand of the NR Group, was started in 1948 by Arjuna Ranga Rao's grandfather N Ranga Rao. The companycreates its own fragrances and has around 500 of them. Owning a 20-22% market share with a turnover of 12 billion, maintaining their market leadership for over 40 years. The brand also has associations with cricket.

Another company under the NR Group is Ripple Fragrances. It is led by Arjun's cousin Kiran Ranga. And now there are many more.

The family was very clear that when people of the third generation came in, they would each head a different company.

Though the group could have easily ended up as yet another small-scale agarbatti manufacturer, they have managed to avoid the pitfalls of family businesses and have been successful in motivating the next generation to start their own business rather than divide the existing pie.

This same drive brought Vishnu Ranga, Kiran's brother, back into the business too.

Vishnu handles Vyoda (an agri-tech startup) and Senzopt (a company in the IoT space).

With a large family and so many diverse businesses and business verticals under the group, succession planning is paramount for them.

Succession Planning

The second generation, alongside building and expanding the business, was prudent enough to understand the critical importance of succession planning.

"Realising that planned Succession was the mantra to avoiding conflict, Both Murthy and Guru Ranga, chairman of NR Group, began attending succession planning seminars or workshops. In fact, Murthy encouraged both Arjun and Pavan, too, to attend similar workshops at Harvard."

They also made the crucial decision of not having two family members in the same company when the third generation came in.

With proper succession planning in place, this diverse family and business group has managed to avoid bitterness and battle and continues to grow from strength to strength.

Source: Forbes India

Two Families running One Family Business!

–EMAMI GROUP

The Emami Group, owned and managed by two Marwari families from Kolkata, has many secrets behind its success. However, the secret ingredient in the recipe for success was the friendship between R.S Agarwal, 77, and cofounder and co-chairman Radhe Shyam Goenka, 76.

They have been life-long friends. In the sixties, in order to spend more time with each other, they started a new venture together. Friends since school, they both went on to become chartered accounts and had separate jobs. To spend even more time together, alongside their jobs in 1968, they started a cosmetics business.

The business kept growing in size, but the duo ensured that the two clans bonded like families at work and in their personal space. R.S. Agarwal had taken Goenka under his wing right since their school days, and that dynamic has stayed strong till today. Bothfamilies say that they have all accepted RS Agarwal as their leader.

Currently, there are quite a few members of both families from the next generation in key positions in the business. The shadow of Succession looms large on the horizon, and soon the bonding of the Emami Groupis likely to be put to the test.

Right now, there are nine members of the two families working together in the top management. However, due to the acceptance of R.S Agarwal as the undisputed leader, there are quick resolutions to most disagreements.

Though Goenka's youngest brother Sushil is the managing director, a bulk of the executive powers are vested with RS Agarwal and RS Goenka.

There is a clear division of responsibility among key family members. The second generation was encouraged and groomed to join the business early. They would come to the office after school and college and be given small tasks like dispatch, couriers and even post office work. The tradition has continued till the third generation.

The group also ensures bonding through family activities such as the practice of the joint working lunch that every working family member attends at the Emami headquarters in Kolkata.

Additionally, they have set up a business council, and the group's professional chief executives and family members jointly sit together on this council to take significant decisions.

At the family council, all the near about 60 family members meet and discuss important matters and bond together through joint vacations and festivities. They generally book resorts and stay together indoors playing cards and sharing jovial companionable meals. In a unique tradition, one meal is cooked by the men during the vacation. Everyone participates in this.

They tried to avoid divisiveness by forbidding things such as buying expensive cars or other forms of showing off. Cars are allotted to members by the family's basis their needs. It is forbidden for any family members to give unsecured loans or make investments in businesses outside the group.

Like Goenka and Agarwal, the second generation, Manish Goenka and Aditya Agarwal were classmates and benchmates in school and college. Today they have moved out of the flagship company to handle the new businesses of paper, cement, ballpoint pen tips, healthcare, pharmacy, edible oil and retail.

How the families will work out succession planning and manage the future of the group is uncertain as yet. Apparently, the second generation did try to discuss it, but nothing could be concluded to satisfaction. They accept it is a sensitive issue, and the younger generation is willing to let the seniors handle the issue.

Each person from the 3rd generation has specific and substantial roles assigned to them. However, the fact that there is no one clear leader among them and that they are of the same age almost and joined the business also at the same time could prove to be a challenge in the game of Succession.

It appears possible that strategic diversification could be an amicable tool to manage the future.

The Emami Group has clearly emerged as a diversified player. The group turnover was around 15,000 crore in 2017-18, and EmamiLtd's turnover was 2,530 crore.

It is to be noted that the other businesses of the group are not subsidiaries of Emami Ltd. Instead, they are all directly owned by the promoters. This in itself could be a broad succession plan– an independent business for every member of the two families.

Source: Economic Times

Glossary

1. **Family Succession** - Transitioning of ownership and responsibilities in the family to their successor.

2. **Business Succession** - Transitioning of management & responsibilities in the business to the next person.

3. **Will** - Document expressing one's wishes for the distribution of their assets and liabilities after their demise.

4. **Legacy** - Something that is passed on, whether monetary or non-monetary. It can be one's faith, ethics and core values, assets, etc.

5. **Ownership** - It is a legal right to possess something/power or control over something. In the case of a company, the shareholders have ownership of the company.

6. **Management** - Persons governing the processes through which goals are achieved. In the case of a company, the Directors and other KMPs form its management.

7. **Board of Directors** - Group of people in a company, who represent and work in the interests of the shareholders.

8. **Estate Equalization** - It is the process where the value of the inheritance is transferred in equitable value amongst all the beneficiaries.

9. **Future Proof** - The process of anticipating the future and developing methods of minimising the effects of shocks and stresses of future events.

10. **Family Council** - A meeting of family members at a routine time and place, to discuss and implement important decisions.

11. **Family Constitution** - A document which guides the family's core values, strategy, rules and governance structure for directing the family's affairs.

12. **Family Trust** - A private trust created for the benefit of one's family members.

13. **Gift Deed** - An agreement expressing a person's wish to gift his possessions to another.

14. **Relinquishment Deed** - Legal document expressing their want to give up their rights and claims.

15. **Family Settlement** - Cordial and mutual agreement between the members of a family regarding the distribution of assets of the family.

16. **Shareholder Agreement** - A contract that regulates the relationship between the shareholders and the corporation.

17. **Code of Conduct** - These are the defined set of rules, principles, values, behaviours, etc., that a business considers important and necessary for its functioning. These can be both for the family as well as the business.

Notes:

Notes:

Notes: